HELL IS A WOMAN

Abiathar Zadok

NATIONAL LIBRARY OF NIGERIA CATALOGUING-IN-
PUBLICATION DATA

ZADOK, Abiathar

HELL IS A WOMAN

Nigerian drama (English)

Published in Nigeria by

StyleCom ventures
+234-08023143990, +234-07081579321

PR 9387. 7.Z17H476   2011   822

ISBN: 978-978-48459-3-9 (pbk)   AACR2

Cover design: Bonaventure Zirra

I like the style of dialogue
The strong give and take
Shows strong artistry.
After the first reading,
I promised myself to read it again.
        -Ropo Ewenla

The language is also full of poetry which reveals the
poetic prowess of the author...suspense which is one
of the beauties of drama has been wonderfully used.

Zadok takes control of the mind of his readers
And does with it as he pleases. He has gained
Mastery of taking his readers on a merry-go-round
and delivering them safe at a particular destination
with each of them wanting more of his writing skills
in order to quench their yearning for more acts and
scenes
        - Leadership Newspapers (Kuni Tyessi)

The woman in the play is a symbolic reflection of a
people, not a sex.
        -Saturday Sun (Irene Chidinma Nwoye)

DEDICATION

To the blessed memory of late Godwin Bassey; a friend who had
looked forward to holding a copy of this play in his hands.

CHARACTERS

BOBBY   PEACE'S LOVER
PEACE   BOBBY'S LIVE IN LOVER
MUSA   BOBBY'S FRIEND
BOSE   PEACE'S FRIEND
ALHAJI KOLA   PEACE'S MAN FRIEND
QUEEN   BOBBY'S WIFE
HELEN   BOBBY AND PEACE NIEGHBOR
ALOA   =
AMAKA   =
MAMA PEJU   =
D.P.O   DIVISIONAL POLICE OFFICER
SERGENT   =
CONSTABLE   =
OFFICERS   =

FIRST STAGED BY THE THEATRE ARTS DEPARTMENT
OF THE UNIVERSITY OF ABUJA IN 2011, DIRECTED
BY
DR. EMEM OBONGUKO.

HELL IS A WOMAN

Act 1 Scene 1

SETTING
At dawn. Helen in a faded nightgown and Amaka in a
wrapper knotted above her breast. The ladies are
fetching water from a tap in the compound.

Helen: Good morning.

Amaka: Good morning my sister, hope you had
a peaceful night?

Helen: It was peaceful, thank you. Yours?

Amaka: Peaceful indeed! You mean you have
lived long on this battlefield that
gunshots are now commonplace?

Helen: Oh no! I heard no gunshots. Last night?

Amaka: How could you? When you put on your
headphones and get buried in your
world of books you do not care what
goes on in your neighbourhood.

Helen: Don't tell me robbers came around
here. Ah God! I hope they did not enter
your room?

Amaka: I am not talking about robbers. Well!
Come to think of it, there is no
difference. Your friend (*she point at the
direction of Bobby's room*) is at it again.

Helen: Oh! Is that it? (*Sighs*) there is nothing
new she can do to ruffle my feathers.
What is it this time?

Amaka: Don't say that, she keeps raising the
stakes every day. Last night could not
have been scripted even as a fairy tale.

1

Helen:	Oh yeah?
Amaka:	Some have their livers made of steel.
Helen:	I can't stand the suspense. Give it to me.
Amaka:	You don't understand. I am overwhelmed.
Helen:	Sure!
Amaka:	Your friend brought a lover home and locked Bobby out.
Helen:	Is that news? Have you not seen that times and again?
Amaka:	I mean this time she locked him out for the night.
Helen:	It's a lie! Tell me you are joking.
Amaka:	I wish I were.
Helen:	Holy madness! So what happened?
Amaka:	That was what happened. What do you mean what happened?
Helen:	I mean what did Bobby do when she refused to let him in?
Amaka:	He banged on the door for hours until it dawned on him that she was not opening the door.
Helen:	Then?
Amaka:	What do you expect? He slept by the gate.
Helen:	Tell me something!
Amaka:	He should have gone somewhere to sleep.
Helen:	You mean he did not pull down the door and give her and her man friend a lesson for life?
Amaka:	Lesson indeed.

2

Helen:	Bobby is too weak for my liking.
Amaka:	The guy just left few minutes ago and Bobby has gone in to dress for work.
Helen:	It's a lie!
Amaka:	There might be a storm brewing in there now.
Helen:	Knowing Bobby, I will not bet on it.
Amaka:	What! With the humiliation and inconvenience?
Helen:	Don't get your hopes high.
Amaka:	Aloa was mad. But there was nothing he could do. This house was agog.
Helen:	I missed the trills.
Amaka:	It was a pitiful sight. I felt like vacating my room for him.
Helen:	Ah! That would have been your undoing.
Amaka:	Abi?
Helen:	You would have bitten more than you could chew.
Amaka:	The girl is mad.
Helen:	She needs a match, someone that can relate with her madness for madness. Bobby is soft for her.
Amaka:	Was it not better when she sleeps with her 'clients' in the room while he waits in the sitting room? At least it leaves us speculating things. But to make a public show of it is another thing.
Helen:	There is no difference, secret sin or public scandal.

Amaka:	Why don't you talk to her? She is your friend.
Helen:	Don't step on my nerves. Stop calling her my friend. Granted I identify with the fact that she does not care what anybody's opinion is about her. But her wildness is far beyond my imagination.
Amaka:	I better get ready for work.
Helen:	Yes, let's keep pace with the day

Exits Amaka and Helen with their buckets of water.

End of scene.

Act 1 Scene 2

At the office, it is the end of a working day. Bobby does not seem to be in a hurry to leave and there is no obvious task for him at hand.

Musa:	Where are the stars shining tonight?
Bobby:	Do the stars still shine where you live?
Musa:	I gather the world still rotates round...
Bobby:	That is a fantasy of books.
Musa:	Why do you sound like the sun has robbed you of life?
Bobby:	The sun would have been more merciful to me than the horrors of knowing hell alive.
Musa:	Tell me brother; is life so unfair?
Bobby:	Who talks about fairness? Is it not my lot to embrace cruelty with smiles?
Musa:	Since when has cruelty been the new name of love which you so strongly profess?
Bobby:	Surely you have not invited yourself upon my company to inflict fresh torture on faded fashion.
Musa:	Faded fashion you say? When has love gone out of season?
Bobby:	Love brewed through artificial process breeds hate. Hatred of the highest kind is my new friend and companion.
Musa:	How so soon do the North and South Poles swap places?

5

Bobby: How so difficult do women breathe in and out. I live at the darkest side of the night where no star dares to shine.

Musa: Then shall I join the Salvation Army to rescue you from the clutches of gloom. So tell me in exact terms what ails you brother? Certainly Peace cannot produce such sourness.

Bobby: That name is the coven of evil, where the cauldron of wickedness breeds infestations of calamities unimaginable. I beg of you surrogate brother do not repeat that name except for the invocation of horror.

Musa: How so soon are the tables turned, that love once pure and divine is now cruel and evil?

Bobby: The bitter cup from which I drink has a long trace in roots.

Musa: To return the sun on my brother's face, I will travel the length.

Bobby: Don't let my mood swing bother you. It's nothing serious that bothers me.

Musa: I read the page of your face brother. I wish the verdict of your voice moved me. But your face, and I believe it, tells me otherwise.

Bobby: Alright! If you must know, a matter of no consequence bothers me.

Musa: And this matter you speak of relates to her whose name I must not repeat?

Bobby: You tell me, since you can read my soul.

Musa: If I could read your soul I would pluck
off your dark clouds. In a brother's
place I choose to be worried where you
are concerned.

Bobby: Truly, you've been brotherly than a
blood brother. And I am not
ungrateful. But should my burden weigh
you down?

Musa: Gladly would I carry your cross as mine.
When our benefactor put your hands in
mine and placed on my shoulders
brotherly responsibility, I pledged to pay
back by looking after you. I have no
blood brother but you. We shall travel
together as long as life gives us lease.

Bobby: Very well then. I will tell you my plight.

Musa: Not here. Not now. Not in a hurry.

Bobby: Why? Name the place and time.

Musa: Our favourite spot at Surulere. We drive
there from here.

Bobby: Not a bad idea.

Exit Bobby and Musa.

7

Act 1 scene 3

Musa and Bobby at a clubhouse in Surulere with plates of pepper soup and drinks in the early hours of darkness.

Bobby: Fate brought us together. Having similar backgrounds I took it upon myself to save her from an overbearing taskmistress in my former neighbourhood. When I first saw her, I recognized a replication of the unfortunate circumstances I was just emerging from. I felt her pain for mine and understood her unexpressed anguish. A peasant daughter of crab hunting parents, her cousin brought her to Lagos for greener pastures but instead reduced her to a subhuman life. In my case, my aunt brought me to Lagos on the demise of my sire with a promise of quality education. In her house I neither saw quality nor education. Until divine orchestration propelled a lady in my aunt's environs who had observed with dismay the despicable treatment meted out to me day after day. Like a thief in the night, the lady stole me to the kind hearted Ms Yvon, who loved me not less than my mother would and gave me the treasures of education. Her benevolence brought me to the society of better men.

Musa: You speak of things I know. Tell me what I don't know.

Bobby: If you must know the son, it is good you know the father as well.

Musa: Go way back to the grandfather if it will loosen the grip of sadness on your soul.

Bobby: Of such prescription, I am uncertain. But the bullets that pierce my heart stings betrayal. Having identified her situation as one and the same as mine before I met Ms Yvon, I saw in her a sister that must be emancipated. From comforting her and encouraging her whenever chance brought us together, we plotted her road to freedom. I secured a new accommodation in a different part of town few months to the expiration of my tenancy and moved her there weeks ahead of my relocation. Having noticed the nursing profession has a compelling appeal on her, I was able to arrange for her to train as an auxiliary nurse, and got her a place to work in a hospital.

Musa: The second plate of my pepper soup is fast running out. Your background picture is well painted. Where are you hurting?

Bobby: I will give it to you in a scoop; I love her like no other. She loves me like loving a leper.

Musa: Why do you think so?

9

Bobby: I have gone beyond the realm of thinking. I have finally established the facts for myself.

Musa: Then, let the evidence speak.

Bobby: Where do I hit it from? They abound the files of my sorry experiences. Were I to keep accounts the Atlantic would be a child's play. Let me startle you for starters. Do you know that the loan I took from the office last month was as a result of pressure for me to source money from whatever source?

Musa: Pressure from whom?

Bobby: Who else? My self-inflicted cancer. She made me believe her mother was to undergo a surgical operation back home. Only for me to discover that the money was actually given to her unemployed boy friend for up keep. She has turned my house to a mini brothel, sleeping with men of all shades.

Musa: No, you must be exaggerating that last bit. It is preposterous to say the least.

Bobby: Did I just sense a note of doubt in your voice?

Musa: Let's say I find it hard to believe that the girl you picked from the clay and gave a future will have the guts to go half the way you just described.

Bobby: All you have to do is come around and ask any of my neighbours what manner of a person she turned out to be.

Musa:	Your neighbours know about this?
Bobby:	It is an open secret. She is not discreet about it and owes no one an apology.
Musa:	Forbearance has reached its zenith and forgiveness end of the road. You are not Christ to die for her. She should leave your house immediately.
Bobby:	She is a bird without feathers. Where will she go?
Musa:	Why should that be any concern of yours? Didn't you just say she has a chain of men friends? No, let's put it better. She brings men to nurse in your house. God! How could you put up with such trash?
Bobby:	Easy man, you are raising your voice...
Musa:	I feel like thundering!
Bobby:	Just the way I feel. Agreed, she has infringed on my privacy and pride as a man. But must I push her into the arms of cold and danger? Certainly there must be a better way.
Musa:	Yes, there are a million different ways. And one is that she gets you dead before you are through thinking of a way out.
Bobby:	Why are you such a pessimist?
Musa:	Why are you so blind to life?
Bobby:	What you call blindness is the expression of my faith in her ability to become a better person.
Musa:	Why would you insist on redeeming someone God has given up on? Such an

	ingrate and a disgrace to womanhood, can only unleash on you terrors freshly invented in hell.
Bobby:	If I consign her soul to the devil, would that be a cure? Would peace not desert me with the wings of an eagle?
Musa:	Perhaps you are right. To stay alive with a permanent smile caved on your face, I suggest you acquire a heart of steel and discard the flesh. Pursue blindness like wisdom and close your ears to the amorous sounds of her despicable deeds…
Bobby:	With my own hands I knotted a cobra on my loins for a belt.
Musa:	Let the sucker leave. Out with the flames of charismatic witchcraft, I will hunt her like a rat and throw her out of your house and life.
Bobby:	I crave for patience brother. Would cruelty force barbarism on the tribe of the civilised? No. Let's take the medical approach. Allow the cancer to fully mature, then you cut it off.
Musa:	A very risky thing to do. I support the medical approach, but not your treatment. The only treatment I know for cancer is to arrest it before it spreads. Send her packing tonight.
Bobby:	I will set the process in motion right away.
Musa:	It needs no process, just do it.

Bobby: I will go about it.

Musa: The sooner, the better for your sake.

End of scene

Act 1 Scene 4

At the reception desk of a private hospital, dressed in the white uniform of nurses, Bose is admiring the stones Peace is wearing in her ears.

Bose: You are lucky. He is really taking good care of you.

Peace: You sound as if he has a choice.

Bose: What do you mean he doesn't have a choice? Does any string bind him to you?

Peace: That would have been very easy. You see, Bobby is mine for as long as I need him.

Bose: I've had stories of lovers using voodoo on their partners I never believed them.

Peace: Ah! Watch your tongue. You went before the gun. I don't do voodoo.

Bose: Then you are taking him for granted.

Peace: Thanks Miss Concerned. May be if I don't know Bobby like I know my fingers, I might share your sentiments.

Bose: Don't be very sure. Men can spring surprises when you least expect.

Peace: Well! Not the type of Bobby.

Bose: Am I missing something? What type is he?

Peace: He is the type that runs on his heart in the place of his head.

Bose: That my dear, is the deadliest class. When they snap they take no hostages.

14

Peace:	Save your theories for your skin. Bobby is a fish in my frying pan.
Bose:	You don't cease to amaze me Peace. How can you say that of a man who has done so much for you?
Peace:	Do you know your problem? You close your eyes when you should open them.
Bose:	Meaning?
Peace:	You experience heartbreaks because you are as docile as Bobby. Why is it so difficult for you to learn a thing or two from me? In case you have forgotten, Bobby is a man. And all men are slippery. Every woman in the life of a man is like a flower in season, once your season is over, you should be grateful to be remembered as part of history. That is why I will skim the cream of his large heart. By the time he is through with me, I would have been twice through with him.
Bose:	That is the point I am making. You don't need such evil schemes. He wants to marry you. What else do you want?
Peace:	Hear yourself: (*she mimics Bose*) he wants to marry you what else you do want? Nonsense. I want financial freedom first before any other thing.
Bose:	After financial freedom what next, will you marry your money?
Peace:	First things first. I like that saying

Bose: Listen to me, accept his proposal and fix a date. No man will love you like he loves you.

Peace: You don't know that yet. But wait a minute. Are you jealous?

Bose: You know what? If I were in your position I would treat Bobby like the precious treasure that he is.

Peace: That will be your undoing. Men never like arrivals, once they think they have conquered you, they look for another challenge to conquer. They are restless by nature. To keep any of them that I find useful, I keep him busy.

Bose: Don't you see the danger of that? You could lose him to the arms of another woman.

Peace: Like you?

Bose: Please spare me.

Peace: You don't deny it, do you? Come on admit it you have a crush on my Bobby, don't you?

Bose: I will tell you one thing that I have told you before. If I were you I will marry Bobby.

Peace: Are you saying this because you think he bought me the stones I am wearing? Let me let you in on something. Bobby's salary can't fix my hair, do my pedicure and manicure or buy the cream I use on frequent basis. Think straight Bose, there has to be an extra source of

	income. The earrings you just spoke about are worth more than our combined salaries for three months.
Bose:	Peeaaccceee!
Peace:	What is it?
Bose:	I don't understand.
Peace:	What don't you understand? That I use what I have to get what I want?
Bose:	You mean you do calls?
Peace:	I like the way you put it. You make it sound like a communication business. At least I don't hawk my wares on the streets like those cheap girls do.
Bose:	God! Did I hear you right?
Peace:	Yes. So what?
Bose:	I can't see the difference.
Peace:	It will amount to expecting too much from you. I know you are blind.
Bose:	But what about Bobby? You stay together don't you?
Peace:	And so what? He is a means to an end.
Bose:	A means?
Peace:	Stop being naïve! Must everything be spelt out for you? Okay this is it. He pays the rent, settles the bills and brings food home. Must I mention the pocket money and other benefits? That is what he is there for.
Bose:	But that is not fair. Don't you have a conscience?

Peace:	Conscience my dear Bose is a luxury I can't afford. Have you forgotten your encounter with your last boy friend?
Bose:	I don't see how the two episodes relate. Remember I gave him my heart and he tore it to pieces.
Peace:	Exactly my point. I am not giving any man my heart so I won't experience heartbreak.
Bose:	You are callous.
Peace:	Your opinion doesn't matter.
Bose:	So tell me, what matters?
Peace:	My swelling bank account.
Bose:	Money is not everything you know?
Peace:	I have heard the poor console each other with that line. Enough of your endless questions, it is almost closing time I better get ready for my date (*she brings out a makeup kit and went to work on her face*).
Bose:	Umh!
Peace:	Oh yeah! The guy is loaded. He works with Shell.
Bose:	So this Shell guy, what is his level?
Peace:	What do you mean level?
Bose:	I mean how do you rate him? Is he marriage material, just fun or what?
Peace:	You really don't understand. He doesn't have a level. Only his money is rated and I can tell you, he is very generous.
Bose:	Poor Bobby! Is he aware?

18

Peace:	Now that you know, you can tell him. And you know what? You can have him when I am through with him.
Bose:	Thanks but no.
Peace:	I thought you have learnt your lesson.
Bose:	I have, Peace.
Peace:	You have not, Bose. If you had, you will not relate to men with your heart but your head (*she taps her head with a finger*).
Bose:	I hope I never get there.
Peace:	Sure? You just made me feel like inviting you to one of my shows with Bobby so you can pick a thing or two.
Bose:	Really?
Peace:	Serious.
Bose:	Show indeed. Sounds interesting, what will the gate fee be?
Peace:	For you, Free.
Bose:	I can't wait. When will this show take place?
Peace:	When Bobby comes out of the shock of being locked out of the house, I will give him another shocker.
Bose:	You locked him out?
Peace:	Yes.
Bose:	In his house? Are you crazy?
Peace:	What do you expect? I had a guest.
Bose:	And that gave you the audacity, temerity, and impetus to lockout Bobby in his own house? Peace you have gone way too far.

Peace: Would you have preferred he witness the act?

Bose: You are disgusting, inhuman and ungrateful.

End of scene.

Act 2 Scene 1

Bobby's room. Bobby has finished packing Peace's belongings in three bags and waits for her to return home.

Bobby: (*Pacing the sitting room, rehearsing how the news will be given to her*) Peace, I have had enough. I have also helped you pack your things, so just go. No! No! That is not good enough. Maybe I should tell her I am married and the wife is coming tomorrow. No, Peace will not buy that. I will just tell her; go. Whatever be the case, Peace will not pass the night under this roof.

Enters Peace

Peace: (*Surprised at the bags in the sitting room and Bobby's expression*) what is happening?

Bobby: Uhmmm! (*Stammers*) Well, this is the end of the road. The calabash is shattered beyond repairs. I mean the cup of endurance overflows. And patience cannot go beyond the wall.

Peace: In simple language what are you saying?

Bobby: Don't play dumb with me. Peace, I wished it would never come to this. It is time to say good-bye. You have to go.

Peace: You have a weird sense of humour Bobby. That's why I love you.

Bobby: You are making light of it. This is no joke and don't try to patronize me.

Peace: Okay you are not joking, fine. Can we sit down and talk about this?

21

Bobby: Sorry, there is nothing to talk about. Just take your bags and go.

Peace: Now I know you are clowning.

Bobby: I don't want to throw your things out, don't make me do it.

Peace: You can't even try it.

Bobby: Don't push me.

Peace: When you are through with your acting please bring my bags back to the room (*she attempts to walk pass him into the room*).

Bobby: Good riddance to … (*he pushes her in the direction of the entrance*).

Peace: Okay, don't push me. I will go this very night on one condition.

Bobby: You are in no position to state any condition.

Peace: If you believe what you just said, you will be the greatest fool God has ever created. But I know you are not stupid.

Bobby: Insult me all you want. That is what I get for nurturing a snake.

Peace: Keep your snake to yourself. I need to rest.

Bobby: You can only find rest outside that door. I have tried to be as gentle as I can, but you…

Peace: I have been trying to tell you something, but you are not listening. If one of us is leaving this house tonight, it will be you.

Bobby: Aha! Are you mad?

Peace: You must be familiar with the symptoms. For your information, I have changed by mind. I will go. But you have to take me back to where you picked me. You will then confess to the crime of kidnapping me, and having me locked up here under your spell. You obviously had me fatten to be trafficked. Thank God your spell has lost its potency before you perpetrate your evil machinations and you are suddenly uncomfortable that I am back to my senses. From my cousin's place, we will go to the police. Let's go.

Bobby: You are out of your senses.

Peace: No. I have just regained sanity. Please you are wasting my time, lets-go.

Bobby: I am not going anywhere.

Peace: It is a lie. You must take me back. I will scream. I will shout. Human trafficker, you must take me back.

Bobby: Please Peace your noise will attract people here.

Peace: If you don't want me to make noise take me back to my people. I want to go.

Bobby: Okay! Because it is late now let's address the issue tomorrow.

Peace: No. I will not sleep in this house tonight.

Bobby: Please Peace, (goes on his knees) I beg of you. Please.

End of Scene

Act 2 Scene 2

Cluster of women in the compound discussing by the tap.

Amaka: Ah! She could kill him oh.

Helen: Nobody should blame her that is what he wants.

Mama Peju: Make una no talk like that oh, na love de shack am.

Amaka: Love ko, love ni.

Mama Peju: You no know say love fit make person de do like say e mumu?

Amaka: (*Erupts into laughter*) if person no mumu, love no fit make am mumu.

Helen: I agree with you. Love cannot make you what you are not out of the blues.

Mama Peju: Na small pikin dey worry una. Una never see correct love wey de make fish live for land. Which one you come dey talk about blues abi na music we de talk for here?

Amaka: Helen rap no bi the blues wey dem de dance. She mean say na so broda Bobby bin dey tey-tey.

Mama Peju: Eh? Which one she come dey sef? Abi you dey support wetin your eyes dey see?

Helen: I don't have to take sides in the matter. The truth is, as bad as we think Peace is, there are men that are worse than her in relationships with women like us.

Amaka: So all you see is the battle of the sexes.

24

Helen:	Not really. I don't envy Bobby, nor do I completely blame Peace.
Mama Peju:	How you go blame her no bi your friend she bi?
Helen:	Does she have a friend in the universe?
Mama Peju:	Na only you no know say she no go university? No bi that apprentice nurse wey Bobby put her she take dey make shakara.
Helen:	I did not make any reference to university education. One wonders why a pot should call a kettle black.
Mama Peju:	Na 'im make I no dey like to carry my matter join with you. You go de bring something wey no surpose dey with wetin people dey talk. Wetin university com do with black kettle for this matter.
Amaka:	Mama Peju, make you no just mind her jo. Okay, dis tin wey you talk now now, so na true say she be ehm house girl before.
Mama Peju:	The time when he carry am come this compound she no dey look people for eye. She de doobale greet people well well. Now wen you meet am for road, if you no comot triela go jam you.
Amaka:	So she be mugu when she bin come?
Mama Peju:	Proper one. Wetin you de talk? You sabi pig wey dey just comot from mud? Na so she bin dey.
Helen:	And then she was well behaved?
Mama Peju:	Well well. Her obey no get part two.

25

Helen: At what point then did she change?

Mama Peju: Na the time when she begin do nurse work, na ehm she begin point finger.

Amaka: Wetin I wan know be say when Bobby see say she don change, wetin him do?

Mama Peju: Wetin you wan make 'im do? E fit no notice sef until yawa come gas.

Helen: Imagine the way she talks to him in public.

Amaka: Na dat one you de talk?

Mama Peju: The thing wey my eyes don see for dis house, I never see am before. I weak, the day when she bring another man come lock Bobby for outside. E knock door tire she no open. E call, call call she no answer. E put ehm key, door no open. E go tanda for gate like say e bi security, before e come go somewhere sleep.

Amaka: That one na later later. the time when she wan begin to de bring men, she talk say na emotional therapy dem de do. broda Bobby go dey for parlour, dem go dey do therapy for room.

Mama Peju: Na true you talk. Na that time him de cry like small pikin.

Helen: Why is he still keeping her?

Mama Peju: E don tire for her. E try pursue her she no gree go.

Helen: He is not serious. I don't think he knows what he wants.

Mama Peju: Ah! No talk so. Just pray make bad luck no bring human devil jam you. Peace don swear say she no de go. She say na Bobby go commot leave her for him house.

Amaka: Aha! When did that happen?

Mama Peju: Dey there. Even sef, (*she looks around*) she don tell Bobby say if him no dey careful she go tell police say him kidnap her.

Helen: What is the meaning of that?

Mama Peju: E never finish. E say Bobby bin wan use her for woman traffic. Na as him juju break she come de do nurse work.

Helen: Human traffic?

Amaka: Nonsense. Since the juju break why she still dey here?

Mama Peju: She no get place to go.

Amaka: See person wey God don butter her bread, she dey take sand pour for her gari.

Mama Peju: Na so life bi oh!

Helen: But how do you come about all these details?

Mama Peju: Sure? You no know say wall get ears?

Amaka: Alao can never take such nonsense.

Mama Peju: Your husband? That one na ogbologbo. He go pound you like pounded yam any day you try it.

Amaka: I put pot for fire jare.

Mama Peju: Make I carry my water de go too.

End of Scene.

27

Act 2 Scene 3

Bobby and Musa in the office

Musa: I see the beauty of the new dawn blaze around you in full blast.

Bobby: I doubt faint eyes could tell the true colours of the sun.

Musa: Like the chameleon changing with the weather, colour is not the issue as long as the sun serves its purpose.

Bobby: Purposes are better served when the skins of men are intact upon their limbs.

Musa: Life is not a planed series of events brother. But tell me, how did the venture go?

Bobby: There was no venture except the trauma of the depressed. The prey has taken the hunter in chains.

Musa: How strange. Is that the progress of the process?

Bobby: The process lasted five seconds. The lamb has caught the lion.

Musa: Bravo! This is the day I dreamt of. At last her animalistic tendencies were curbed by your gentle approach. Kudos to your tactics, I can't wait for the details.

Bobby: Sorry to disappoint you. My one time tenant is now my landlady. Henceforth I do only as she instructs or risk going to jail.

Musa:	By God! Some joke. How is it that the road to emancipation would lead further to captivity?
Bobby:	Last night brought it home to me like never before the fact that wars are not won on drawing boards.
Musa:	How did the revelation come?
Bobby:	Peace painted a picture clearer than the sun. She would leave when rivers stop running.
Musa:	Didn't you ask her for ghost tears in a bottle?
Bobby:	She wills the direction of the wind.
Musa:	Interesting! She is deluding herself thinking she can negotiate? What are the colours of her hallucinations?
Bobby:	The head of John the Baptist.
Musa:	Herodias had that. She can have his umbilical cord. Or did her dreams run in the sun?
Bobby:	If I had it, she won't have it.
Musa:	Very strange; grass eating the horse.
Bobby:	I am up to date, I can tell you the world now revolves in reverse.
Musa:	Feed me the devils request.
Bobby:	It was anything but a request. I am accused of kidnapping her. To flush out the flood of my crime she must ride on my back to the place I picked her from, with a gift of public confession to kidnapping and a documented version to be deposited with the police.

Musa:	Your girl is both amusingly annoying and creatively stupid. What a bluff.
Bobby:	Peace can wobble through a web with such a scheme to make a point.
Musa:	Consummate daughter of hell! For repaying kindness with such evil she will…
Bobby:	Hold your breath, she is not worth cursing.
Musa:	You will rather heaven smile on her?
Bobby:	All the better.
Musa:	Where do we go from here?
Bobby:	With my feet dangling in the clouds, wherever earth offers a landing will be home.
Musa:	How the rampaging storms of hell can eat up a heart so perverse to the extent of strangulating its conscience. Never before has it been said that water flows uphill. For this strange malady there must be a strange treatment.
Bobby:	Tell me the contraptions of your mind.
Musa:	Let air blow on my balding head to draft a ploy that eat up the monster at her own game. The sooner the blood-sucking witch is taken out the better for everyone.
Bobby:	I am sure the blind will see that.
Musa:	That is reassuring. I hope you won't stand in the way of the river.

Bobby:	I don't want to stir the hornet's nest. Let the smoke of the ignited flames blend with the wind.
Musa:	Not this General's idea. In warfare that will give the enemy enough time to perfect a counter attack. We have to keep shooting at full blast to achieve total annihilation.
Bobby:	A General who speaks of battles without experiencing the horrors of one.
Musa:	More than one else you know my pedigree. I never turn my back on a fight.
Bobby:	Incontrovertible as that might be, you have never encountered a formidable foe in the class of Peace.
Musa:	Forgive me. I am blind to what makes her different
Bobby:	She is endowed with schemes inconceivable in the realm of human imagination.
Musa:	Given more time the cancer will only get worst. Are you sure you are not buying time for love?
Bobby:	I remember crossing that mountain.
Musa:	Double checks are not out of place in the face of questionable undertones.
Bobby:	Far as the sky is from the earth, so is my heart from her.
Musa:	Very Well. I will perform the operation. I will cut off the cancer.

Bobby: I do not query your surgical ability, I only wonder what implements you intend to use.

Musa: Don't worry. Capable and meticulous are the hallmarks of your brother. Banish your fears, there will be no accidents.

Bobby: Anxiety not fears have taken roots in my soul. We cannot afford a scandal on any scale.

Musa: It is obvious she has injected you with a lethal dose of contagious fear. She got you exactly where she wants you. But don't worry there will be no haemorrhage.

Bobby: Peace is capable of any imaginable wickedness. A blow out of place could be fatal.

Musa   Reflections of your tortured love life is getting the better part of your reality.

Bobby: Caution is a lifeline, or quicksand will make a meal of you.

Musa: You give her more credit than she deserves.

Bobby: I know the shark in my aquarium. You cannot imagine the extent of her craftiness. She does not miss a good opportunity. She can turn a seemingly disadvantaged situation to her favour.

Musa: If the mountain is unmovable why try at all? Live with the status quo.

32

Bobby:	Given recent events, that will be tantamount to sleeping with a dagger at my throat.
Musa:	Given Peace' intimidating credentials, I will not want to embark on a war against an invincible foe.
Bobby:	Do I smell a crack in audacity? Don't tell me my General is losing steam.
Musa:	I am watching the exhibition of timidity a jaundiced mind is capable of inflicting on a man of your standing.
Bobby:	My offence, for sounding the alarm for your safety. You have dared the dragon. She does not fight fair.

End of Scene.

Act 2 Scene 4

Bobby's sitting room. Musa and Bobby chat excitedly with drinks, after perfecting the strategy to unleash on Peace.

Bobby: Why roll rocks to fill the valley if we can just put her things out and lock the door.

Musa: If the enemy is larger than life why give her such an advantage?

Bobby: She could resort to violence.

Musa: It would be insane to contemplate that.. But if the brand of her madness pushes her to try it, militancy is not her exclusive prerogative.

Bobby: Exactly my fear! Things could go out of hand.

Musa: Things don't just get out of hand.

Bobby: I will hate to watch the two of you exchange punches.

Musa: Restraining her will do, if it comes to that.

Bobby: When the party is over and the dust of the shock settles, I wonder how she will survive it.

Musa: I doubt it will be much of a surprise; you have prepared her enough for the coming storm. She might even have a plan B.

Bobby: Yeah! Like she could carry out her threats?

Musa: Come to think of it, why not confess to the crime of kidnapping?

34

Bobby: The dish of surprise she served was so hot; the heat of it blinded me. It was stupid of me to buy such nonsense.

Musa: She must have a good explanation for leaving the house to work and returning by herself.

Bobby: How come that did not hit me? Well, she had her day. The girl is good. Give it to her.

Musa: The fool will not look a fool while on break.

Bobby: She cannot go to the police with such a story. I was a fool.

Musa: She manipulated you through intimidation and paralysed your thinking.

Bobby: She spins it up in a split of a second and got herself off the hook. So help me God, I will give it back to her.

Musa: Being rash could be costly. You take it calm, slow but firm. That is the hallmark of a man, my brother.

Bobby: Okay! I will take my time. Calm, slow but firm.

Musa: So are the clouds filled with rains. You dispense vengeance with the composure of the aristocracy, which is what class is.

Bobby: So shall it be. But be sure she will not take it laying low.

Musa: By the time she realises the locks have altered appearance, she will know trouble is in the offing. She will not expect the welcome awaiting her until the goods are delivered. Before she gets the import of the message, the war is over. Let's see if she will pull down the door.

Bobby: On this drawing board the war has been won before it started.

Musa: The element of surprise is of utmost importance.

Bobby: The falconer is home to an empty nest. She is in a good mood. Can you hear her singing?

Musa: I hope she will still be singing when it is over.

Bobby: God! My heartbeat is speeding up let this be over fast.

Musa: Calm down. Just stick with your biddings and leave the rest to me.

Enters Peace.

Peace: (*She tries her key on the door and noticed the changed locks. She shakes her head and knocks on the door*) Hello! I am home. Open the door.

Bobby: (*From within*) who are you?

Peace: It's me.

Bobby: Who?

Peace: Aha! What is happening?

Bobby: Can you identify yourself please?

Peace: Okay Bobby, I am Peace. Please open the door. I had a busy day at work I need to rest.

Bobby: Identify yourself properly please. Peace who? And what do you want here?

Peace: What games are you playing?

Bobby: You want me to open the door for you to enter?

Peace: Why all these questions? What is going on?

Bobby: Answer yes or no please if you want me to open the door

Peace: I am very happy today I got a pay raise. So I will play along. Yes I want to come in please open the door for me.

Bobby: Who are you?

Peace: My name is Peace John.

Bobby: What do you want here?

Peace: I live here. How long is this going to last?

Bobby: It's over. Step back let me open the door.

Peace: What was the interrogation all about?

Bobby: You will soon know (*the door opens and two bags flew out. Before the third bag could find its way out, Peace rammed into the sitting room standing with hands akimbo*).

Peace: You will have to kill me. I will not let you embarrass me. I am going nowhere

Bobby: (*To Musa*) did you get everything?

Musa: (*Smiling victoriously*) From Genesis to Revelation.

Peace: (*To Musa*) So you are the one behind the humiliation I was subjected to? (*Turns to Bobby*) Okay I get it. What you could not

	accomplish, you hired a mercenary to do it for you.
Bobby:	You have over stayed your welcome. If I did wrong by helping you, God will judge. Now leave my house.
Musa:	And don't bother trying to sell the kidnap bullshit because I have you on record begging to be admitted in, just in case you are desperate enough to want to try.
Peace:	You will regret this.
Musa:	Do your worse.
Bobby:	Go Peace, go.
Peace:	Bobby!
Musa:	Don't Booby him anything. What part of go do you find difficult understanding? Is it the G or the O?
Peace:	It will serve you better to stay out of this even though we never liked each other from the first day we met.
Musa:	I am glad you know it. I never knew you have the head to notice it.
Peace:	I don't want to engage in verbal exchange this evening. Just know that I am going nowhere. My bags are used to being thrown out and brought back, Bobby will tell you better.
Musa:	Not this time (*He shoves her out with lightening speed she lands on her buttocks outside. The door is locked from within*).
Peace:	Ehee! You don look for trouble find am. Today you will know why I am Peace.

	You laid your hands on me. You dare to beat me? (*She starts rolling on the ground*).
Bobby:	When you have finished exhibiting your madness to the world, you will leave my door.
Peace:	This is just the beginning. You have called for rain and lightning shall strike you.
Musa:	Don't boast of things beyond you, take your bags and leave with what is left of your pride if you have any.
Peace:	Woman beater. You no get shame. Go and find a man like you to fight.

Enters Alao

Alao:	(*Helps Peace to her feet*) No worry, no bi by force. If e say e no do again make you carry your kaya dey waka.
Peace:	Agbero. Na your house go scatter. Na so dem dey settle mater? (*Pushes Alao away*)
Alao:	Shoo! See me see trouble oh. Na today I see say dem dey love by force. If you try abuse me again I go penal beat you sotey your mama no go sabi you.
Peace:	You can't do me anything. You think say I bi dat village girl wey you dey beat anyhow?

Enters Amaka

Amaka:	(*Knotting her wrapper for war*) If you be witch no bring am come my side. If I be

39

village girl, I no be prostitute. Shameless woman. Dem for pursue you tey-tey.

Peace: See you (*points a finger at Amaka*) you think you can stand me? Come closer let me deal with you.

Alao: You don tire everybody for this yard. The cloth wey you take cover him eyes don comot. Carry your wahala de go.

Amaka: (*Mockingly*) No worry I go help you keep your bags until you get place.

Peace: (*Pounding on the door*) Bobby wait for me, I am coming. All of you wait for me I am coming back now. (*She walks towards the gate*).

Alao: You don dey leave your bags behind.

Exit Peace.

Amaka: (*Singing and dancing*) Congratulation, and jubilation, celebration in our compound...'

Enters Mama Peju and others dancing with Amaka in front of Bobby's room.

Musa: Feel the flow in the air, the compound is alive.

Bobby: Lets playback the recording (*picks the tape recorder and begins to play*).

End of scene.

Act 3 Scene 3

Police station. Peace is dirty from rolling on the ground. Her nurse uniform is torn in two places. A plaster covers her left eye. The entire residents of the premises are also present.

Officer 1:   Madam Nurse, what did you say happened?

Peace: (*Sobbing*) I was returning from work and this hired assassin (*points at Musa*) attacked me. You can see the injuries (*points at her face*) it was only God that saved me from him

Officer 2:   (*To officer 1*) that is attempted murder, write it down. (*To Peace*) Yes go on.

Peace: After that this Area Boy (*points at Alao*) pinned me to the ground and tore my uniform and was trying to…

Officer 2:   Don't say it. That is attempted rape. Yes what again?

Amaka: It's a lie.

Officer 2:   Who are you?

Peace: She is the one who took my purse away while I was struggling with her partner in crime.

Office 2:   That is armed robbery. Constable!

Constable: Sir.

Officer 2:   Bring the three criminals this way (*separates them from the others*).

Constable: Yes sir. You, you and you (*points to Musa, Alao and Amaka*) come here.

41

Musa:	This is unacceptable. You cannot treat …
Officer 2:	Shut up. (*Goes to the radio*) S.O to Area Command, S. O to Area Command, Area Command come in, over.
D.P.O:	(*On radio*) Area Command to S.O, reading you loud and clear, over.
Officer 2:	Station update, permission to carry on, over.
D.P.O:	Roja, over.
Officer 2:	We have rounded up a gang of murderers, rapists and robbers. We have commenced interrogation in the station. Reporting for further instruction sir. Over.
D.P.O	Carry on officer. You are walking your way up the ladder. I am on my way, over and out.
Musa:	What kind of police do we have here? You just heard a trumped up accusation and you are acting on it without the slightest investigation not as such as hearing from the other side
Officer 1:	You want to teach me my work? Move this way, criminals. We will rid society of elements like you.
Officer 2:	(*To Officer 1*) If anyone resists lawful arrest, what do you do officer?
Officer 1:	Use reasonable force sir.
Officer 2:	That is correct. Carry on.
Officer 1:	Yes sir.
Officer 2:	Constable.

Constable:	Sir.
Officer 2:	Who are all these people? What do they want?
Peace:	They are the people that joined in beating me.
Officer 2:	Mob action. We will charge them with unlawful assembly and disturbance of public peace.
Mama Peju:	Oga Police how una take know?
Officer 2:	Na our work.
Constable:	How we take know wetin, woman?
Mama Peju:	I surprise as una call am public woman.
Constable:	Nobody said that.
Mama Peju:	Aha! Nobi now, now oga call am Public Peace?
Peace:	Na you, your mama, and your mama him mama be public women.
Mama Peju:	I talk to you? You no dey fear? You craze wey you go abuse my mama? Who born you?
Peace:	Wetin you fit do?
Amaka:	Ashawo.
Helen:	Shameless and ungrateful parasite.
Peace:	Witches. Una plan am before. Take this (*She slaps Mama Peju. A free for all fight ensues*).
Officer 2:	All of you stop that. I said stop it. Constable.
Constable:	Sir.
Officer 2:	Put all of them in cell.
Constable:	Yes sir.
Helen:	You can't do that.

43

Officer 2: Who said that?

Helen: I did (*stepping forward*). What are you detaining us for? And what evidence do you have except for the words of a pathological liar against all of us?

Officer 2: Shut up. Do you know that obstruction of a police officer is a criminal offence? Who are you by the way?

Officer 1: (*Whispers to officer 2*) I think she is a lawyer.

Officer 2: Because you are a lawyer you think your grammar will intimidate me?

Peace: She is not a lawyer, she is a...

Officer 2: So why are you speaking like a lawyer? If you talk like that again, I will charge you for impersonation. Constable.

Constable: Sir.

Officer 2: March them to cell.

Alao: Nobody de go cell. Wetin bi your problem sef? You never ask us any question na soso cell, cell you dey talk. Abi you don collect money from her?

Officer 2: False accusation. You accuse an officer of bribery and corruption?

Musa: Enough of this nonsense. I demand to see the Divisional Police Officer immediately.

Officer 2: I am the officer in charge. Why do you want to see the D. P. O. and who are you?

Musa: You appear to be incapable of handling the simple issue at hand.

Officer 2:	You want to teach me how to conduct investigations? Do you know how long I have been doing this work?
Helen:	You might have been doing the wrong thing.

Enters D. P. O

Officer 2:	Who said that? (*Sees the D. P. O*) Attention! (*All the policemen stamps their feet*). At ease.
D. P. O:	Where are the robbers, rapist and murderers?
Officer 2:	Here (*points at the threesome isolated from the rest*). And these are the rioters, resisting arrests and disturbing public peace.
D.P.O:	Where are the weapons recovered from the robbers?
Officer 2:	Constable, where are the weapons recovered from the robbers?
Constable:	There are no weapons, sir.
Officer 2:	There are no weapons, sir.
D. P. O:	Where were they operating?
Officer 2:	I was told it was at eh ......eh.
Musa:	Excuse me sir.
Officer 2:	Shut up.
D. P. O:	Let him speak.
Musa:	Thank you sir. My name is Musa. I work with Arrow International Limited. My brother there (*points at Bobby*)...
Peace:	You are not related.

45

Musa:	(I*gnoring her*) it is a domestic issue with no link to robbery, rape or murder.
D. P. O:	Officer is that correct?
Officer 2:	No sir. That is not the complaint we received.
D. P. O:	Where is the complainant?
Peace:	I am here.
D. P. O:	What is the matter?
Peace:	I have already made my statement. You can read it if you want. These people are supposed to be in cell. I don't know why you are still keeping them here.
Officer 2:	Answer the question. What is your complain?
Peace:	I have made my statement.
Officer 2:	Make it again.
Peace:	This hired assassin attacked me (*points at Musa*).
D. P. O:	With what?
Peace:	With his hands.
D. P. O:	Be careful young woman, you are making serious allegations here. I hope you can prove them?
Musa:	Oho!
Peace:	Yes. Can't you see my nose?
D. P. O:	Well! Go ahead.
Peace:	The Area Boy (*points at Alao*) attempted to rape me, you can see the way he tore my uniform. While his partner took away my purse.
Amaka:	It is a lie.

Mama Peju:	Oga Poilce this woman (*points at Peace*) na craze-dog, she wan bite her owner.
Helen:	She is an ingrate.
D. P. O:	One person at a time please.
Bobby:	(*Addressing the D. P. O*) Officer, she was staying with me. When living with her became hotter than hell, I asked her to go.
Peace:	I will go. But everybody must pay for the harm done to me.
D. P. O:	Officer
Officer 2:	Yes sir.
D. P. O.:	I am disappointed at the gang you rounded up.
Officer 2:	Sir, they will not confess anything under this cosy circumstance. By the time I introduce them to the interrogation room, they will confess.
DPO:	Release these people and let them go.
Officer 2:	Sir?
D. P. O:	You heard me.
Officer 2:	Yes Sir. Release these people and let them go. I heard you.
All:	Thank you sir.
Mama Peju:	God go bless you jare.

Exits D. P. O

Officer 2:	Ah! Excuse me sir. (*Runs after the DPO*)
Helen:	Can you imagine the way he was going? I will charge you with impersonation. Mob action…

Bobby: Attempted murder

Helen: Armed robbery.

Enters officer 2

Officer 2:   (*Smiling sheepishly*) Ah constable!

Constable: Yes

Officer2:   Release the rioters. The D. P. O is in a good mood today. Everybody go home, except the murderer, robber and rapist'

Amaka: No. The D. P. O said all of us should go.

Peace: Don't release them oh! My life is in danger and you want to release the people threatening my life

Officer 2:   (*To Peace*) look here. I will charge you for false accusation if you speak again. Where are the weapons they attacked you with? If I hear your voice again I will interrogate you personally. (*Turns to Musa, Alao and Amaka*) Do you have someone to bail you out? Or you want to bail yourselves?

Musa: Why do we have a need for bail? The D. P.O said we should go.

Officer 2:   Good! Go let me see.

Booby: I will bail them.

Officer 2:   Good! Stand here. The rest of you I said go home, why are you still here?

Helen: We are waiting for the others. We will go together.

Officer 2: Go home they will join you after our investigation.

Mama Peju: Wetin you want investigate again? Na only you no know say na so-so lie-lie this eh eh dey talk?

Officer 2: Good! Since you don't want to go, Constable bring this woman (*points at Mama Peju*).

Mama Peju: I beg no vex, I dey go. (*Runs out of the station*).

Alao: (*To the rest*) Nothing dey happen. Make una dey go.

Bobby: Go. We will join you soon.

Helen: Officer if you don't release them soon we will come back for you.

Exits Helen, Mama Peju, and Amaka.

Officer 2: Come. (*Leads Bobby to a corner*) eh! You know, bail is free. But the fine for the offences they are charged with is five thousand per head. That is fifteen thousand if you add the nurse that will be twenty thousand.

Bobby: I don't understand what you are saying. Are you asking me for bribe?

Officer 2: God forbid. Didn't I tell you that bail is free? If you don't want to bail them you too can go. Except you want to join them. (*To Peace*) are you ready to bail yourself?

Peace: For what? I am the complainant.

Officer 2:	You brought false accusation against these people.
Peace:	How do you know the accusation is false?
Officer 2:	We don't know yet. That is why we need to detain you while we investigate. Constable, put her in cell.
Peace:	How much is it? I will pay.
Officer 2:	False accusation is ten thousand.
Peace:	Take; (*counting money from her purse*) I have only four thousand.
Officer 2:	It is not enough. But bring it. The police is your friend. (*Collects money*) if any one attacks you again let me know.
Peace:	Nobody will attack me.
Officer 2:	(*To Bobby*) what are you saying?
Bobby:	Here (*Counts some bank notes for the officer*).
Officer 2:	Constable, the D. P. O's instruction is that all of them be released. Release them.

End of scene.

Act 3 Scene 4

Outside the Police Station.

Peace: *(Kneeling in front of Amaka)* I take God beg you, forgive me. Na devil work. Please help me beg your husband and Bobby make dem forgive me.

Amaka: Me wey be robber, na me go forgive you for robbing you again? Nobi you suppose forgive me? E no go better for you.

Peace: Please! This time I know I have gone way beyond the limits. I beg you, have mercy on me. I won't do it again.

Amaka: God punish you.

Peace: No vex, I still dey beg you. Please.

Amaka: Get up. Stand up before you attract attention.

Peace: I will get up when you forgive me.

Amaka: Make you change oh! This attitude no go pay you.

Peace: Yes ma. Thank you very much.

Amaka: Oya get up. I no dey keep person for mind. But I no go talk to Alao or Bobby for you.

Alao: *(Coming out of the station. Surprise to see Peace Kneeling down)* wetin dey happen?

Peace: *(Goes to meet Alao and went on her kneels)* Oga Alao, I take God beg you, forgive me.

Alao: Area Boy don become oga, abi? No bi Area Boy I be?

51

Peace: I beg no put am for mind. Na devil work. Please forgive me. If Bobby pursue me, I no get place to go. Make you no consider my character, forgive me because of God.

Alao: Which one concern agbero for overload? That one na between Bobby and you. My own be say, the rape wey you lie say I bin wan rape you, na now I go do am (*he reaches out to hold her*).

Amaka: (*Prevents him*) Wetin dey do you? Which kind yan be that?

Alao: You dey ask me? You no dey when she tear her cloth say na me tear am sake of say I wan rape her?

Amaka: That one don pass now, she don dey beg you for forgiveness.

Alao: Weyrae dey beg Alaye for forgiveness, I go think am one week before I answer you. But I must rape you oh! Woo, wherever you run go, I go look for you.

Amaka: Which kind talk be that? E don do make we dey go.

Peace: Sorry.

Alao: Tell that to the police. The small money wey you suppose add go find house, you carry dey give police. E don pay you, abi?

Peace: Police no dey pay.

Alao: Shoo!

Peace: I make big mistake. I don repent. Forgi....

Enters Bobby and Musa.

Alao:	(*To Bobby and Musa*) Make una come see oh!
Bobby:	What is it?
Alao:	Peace don born again.
Musa:	Let's go please, it is late.
Amaka:	Na true oh.
Peace:	(*Runs to Bobby and Musa*). Please I know I don't have the right to ask for forgiveness, but find a place in your hearts to forgive me.
Musa:	You don't need it. Go in peace.
Peace:	I know what I did is unpardonable. To think I will be forgiven is madness. But I have no other choice than to ask for forgiveness because the very ground upon which I stand emits repulsion. I have beaten the fingers that feed me. I cannot live with it.
Bobby:	Go. You are forgiven.
Peace:	Forgiveness so cheaply given is no forgiveness at all.
Musa:	It is not the first time, why should it bother you now?
Peace:	It was never this bad.
Musa:	You mean it was never this public. And the resolve to get rid of you was never this strong
Bobby:	(*To Musa*) let's be going. Its late you will pass the night at my place.

Musa:	No. I will still make it to my place; it's just after 10.pm.
Alao:	E betta make you stay give us support for house oh.
Musa:	No. You don't need no further support. The worst has happened.
Bobby:	If you insist we better get a taxi for you then.
Musa:	That will be great for the night. This armed robber woman (*referring to Amaka*) can do with a little rest.
Peace:	(*Clinging to Bobby's feet*) Please let not mercy turn her back on…
Bobby:	You asked for forgiveness, you have been forgiven. What else do you want?
Peace:	(*Crying*) I don't have a place to go.
Bobby:	That is no longer my business. There are hotels all over town.
Musa:	The chain you were hitting with the hammer is broken. You have to find a means of holding your bundle together.
Bobby:	Let go of my legs please.
Peace:	I am undone. Please do not let my stupidity ruin the good you have started.
Bobby:	What good? Thinking I could help you was the worst step I have ever taken.
Peace:	But you helped me. You gave me a life and a future.
Musa:	And you paid back in the best currency you can.

Bobby:	Now I think I will do well to heed the age long saying "God for us all, everyone to himself."
Peace:	Please, Oga Alao help me beg am.
Alao:	Which one be my own? You dey waste our time.
Musa:	Kick her off your feet if she won't let you go.
Amaka:	(*To Bobby*) Allow her to sleep this night…
Musa:	It will be a grievous mistake to even contemplate it.
Bobby:	Henceforth, I am both deaf and blind to the music and colours of mercy.
Amaka:	She may not have money to pay for a hotel accommodation
Bobby:	Accommodate her then.
Amaka:	Where?
Bobby:	Don't you have a house?
Alao:	I go rape am oh!
Musa:	(Laughing). And your wife will rob her.
Amaka:	Make una stop am. Yan serious matter.
Musa:	The serious matter there is right now, is for me to take a taxi home.
Bobby:	This lady is glued to my legs like a leech.
Musa:	I am beginning to think you are enjoying it.
Bobby:	That is not fair.
Musa:	Well! If you think she is going to let go of your legs because you ask pleasantly, you need to wake up, she won't.
Bobby:	I am afraid I could hurt her.

Alao:	Wetin you dey fear, after the yawa wey don gas.
Musa:	Nurture your fears I am out of here.
Alao:	Bros make I help you get taxi jare.
Bobby:	Thanks a million brother, see you at the office tomorrow. (*Bobby extracted himself from Peace' grip and bolted out racing like a bull*)

End of scene

Act 4 Scene 1

Peace and Bose at their duty post in the hospital.

Bose:	Unbelievable! You mean Bobby asked you to leave his house?
Peace:	It is that Mallam in his office that is deceiving him. By the time I am through with both of them, they will prefer boiling oil than my fury.
Bose:	How did it happen?
Peace:	They had everything planned out. A few days ago, I threatened Bobby I was going to report him to the police for kidnapping me when he tried to send me packing.
Bose:	You did?
Peace:	Listen! To counter my threat they recorded my pleadings to be let into the house after having identified myself on tape and all such nonsense.
Bose:	Really!
Peace:	I told you it was planned
Bose:	So how were you told to go?
Peace:	They simply threw out my things and knocked the door against me. Mind you, the locks have been changed before I got home that day.
Bose:	Wahoo! So where did you sleep?
Peace:	Ah! Don't you trust me? I slept in the house.
Bose:	Don't tell me you pulled down the door.

57

Peace:	No. I used womanpower to open the door.
Bose:	How?
Peace:	Ohm. Bose, do you know that when Bobby threw out my things all the witches and wizards in that premises gathered to beat me up?
Bose:	Are you serious?
Peace:	My secret enemies were exposed. I don't have a friend in that compound. Even Helen that pretends to be my friend did not support me. In fact she was on their side at the police station.
Bose:	The matter went to the police?
Peace:	I arranged police for them. The police cleared the entire compound. I acted oh. I cried.
Bose:	You Peace, cried?
Peace:	I cried with real tears. I tore my uniform and told the police Alao tried to rape me. I am sure the police were impressed. I should have been an actress you know?
Bose:	I can imagine. So the police told Bobby not to send you away?
Peace:	No! Bobby is as predictable as a written book. Didn't I tell you I have him in my palms?
Bose:	Ehm!
Peace:	I promised to pack my things and leave the next morning if he would let me

	pass the night. I also promised to roll my waist for him the way he likes it.
Bose:	And did you roll your waist?
Peace:	(*Boastfully*) that is why he can't do without me. As soon I took in my last bag and closed the door, he pounced on me like a hungry lion. In the process he confessed that sending me away was not his idea.
Bose:	You don't mean it!
Peace:	We have reconciled our differences. We woke up on the same bed this morning.
Bose:	Does that mean you are not packing out?
Peace:	Pack out for where? The guy is begging me to stay.
Bose:	Peasoooo! I beg, you will give me the secret.
Peace:	Don't worry. You have enrolled into my army of students.
Bose:	When will lectures start?
Peace:	For starters I give you a free tutorial. Never love a man but use him for what you will get. Example: protection, class, food and money. Lesson two; protect your heart. Three; use your head. Four; shine your eyes. This will do for a certificate course. I will give you a diploma after a practical session in the no distant future.
Bose:	Professor Peace! (*She gives Peace a high five, smiling.*)

End of Scene

Act 4 Scene 2

Musa in the office of Mr. Jude the Head of Admin and Human Resources. Musa is facing Mr. Jude in a cosy and spacious office.

Musa: Sir, I came to see you on an issue of grave concern.

Jude: Okay (*adjusting his glasses*)! What is it about?

Musa: It concerns Bobby.

Jude: Okay, I am all-ears.

Musa: Sir, Bobby needs to relocate from his present accommodation. He is not safe where he is and may not even be aware of the danger.

Jude: How do you know? I mean, what gave you that impression?

Musa: It is a long story sir.

Jude: Make it brief.

Musa: About two weeks ago, I went to help Bobby throw out the hydra-headed monster living with him. After the exercise, she went to the police station and filed a complaint accusing me of attempted murder. Sir, it will amaze you to know that that very night after we parted at the police station, she was able to manipulate Bobby into taking her back. The most heart-renting of all is that she has now brought in a man-friend she claim to be her brother, into

Bobby's house. My sources believe the young man was staying at Costain until he was booted out lately for his inability to renew his rent. But she told Bobby that he came to Lagos for an employment interview. It's close to two weeks now and he is still in the house.

Jude: Do I understand you to mean Bobby is not aware of what you are saying?

Musa: It is either he does not know or, he is not willing to accept it for what it is.

Jude: Well! If he does not know, don't you think he should know?

Musa: It will only make matters worse sir?

Jude: How?

Musa: Sir, the girl is up to a sinister scheme. I must confess that I fear her grip on Bobby is beyond the ordinary.

Jude: Musa, I appreciate your concern for Bobby. But he has his life to live. What if he does not see things the way you do?

Musa: That is exactly my point sir. I am afraid she has manipulated him to the extent that he is not rational where she is the subject.

Jude: Even at that, who made you Mr. Fix it? You said the girl accused you of attempted murder and Bobby is still keeping her. Does that not tell you something?

Musa: Yes sir. It tells me that Bobby is under a spell.

Jude: Now you are speculating. But wait a minute; I hope it's not the same girl he wanted to marry last year.

Musa: We are talking about one and the same person.

Jude: Why is he still keeping her?

Musa: You might want to answer that question sir. The incident you referred to is the least in view of recent events.

Jude: Even at that we don't have the right to invade Bobby's private live without his consent.

Musa: Sir, correct me if I am wrong. Is it not the sick man who knows that he is sick that looks for a cure? Bobby may not know that he needs help.

Jude: I am afraid that makes it even more complex. Unless he request for help, we cannot infringe upon his privacy.

Musa: Sir, I would not have been the one making a case for Bobby. But I am convinced beyond the shadow of a doubt that he needs help. And at the moment sir, I know you are the only person that can help him if you so desire. Please help him sir.

Jude: Well! I will speak with him.

Musa: Thank you sir. I will tell him to see you right away.

Jude: That will be okay.

Exits Musa.
Enters Bobby.

Bobby:	Good day sir. I am told you want to see me.
Jude:	Yes (*adjusting his glasses*). Please take a seat. There are two issues. I have noticed with growing concern the fact that your productivity is constantly advancing on the downward slope. You need to seat up and be focused, okay?
Bobby:	Yes sir.
Jude:	Is there anything getting in the way of your work lately?
Bobby:	No, nothing sir.
Jude:	Okay. I want to see a change.
Bobby:	You will sir, I promise.
Jude:	Okay! The second matter is about your private life. I am sure you understand that you are under no obligation to discuss your private life with anybody. If you choose to discuss your private life with me, it's okay. If on the other hand you decide not to discuss it, it is also absolutely okay. We may care for you as colleagues, but your life is completely your responsibility.
Bobby:	I understand that sir.
Jude:	Okay. Musa told me you are still accommodating that girl who almost wrecked you last year?
Bobby:	I wish I could deny it sir.

Jude:	I understand. You love her in spite of the pains she cause you.
Bobby:	Sir, I am only considering the fact that she has no other place to go.
Jude:	That is very considerate of you. I guess that means you are stuck with each other?
Bobby:	Not exactly sir.
Jude:	No?
Bobby:	Well, I mean…
Jude:	You have given her a start in life. And she won't marry you. She earns a living. Even if you were her father, is she not old enough to fend for herself? Or are you both reconsidering the issue of marriage?
Bobby:	That is a foreclosed issue sir.
Jude:	Then what is the cohabitation about? Are you recouping your investments by that?
Bobby:	Far from it sir. I think having been together for seven years has fostered a companionship I sometimes feel reluctant to let go.
Jude:	You need to move ahead Bobby. Do you understand?
Bobby:	Yes sir.
Jude:	Okay, that will be it.
Bobby:	Thank you sir
Jude:	If there is any way I can be of assistance, do let me know.
Bobby:	That is very kind of you sir.

Act 4 Scene 3

Kola and Sons Contractors office. Alhaji Kola an uneducated contractor is holding a paper.

Kola: Eh! Eh! What is my business with proposal? You think I am interested in moving papers from office to office ke. Just bring the money let us share it as usual. Ole, no bi national cake? If I bring proposal you say I should add hundred percent chop-chop for men and the boys.

Enters Peace.

Peace: Alhaji my love (gives him a peak).

Kola: Eh! Peace or whatever you call yourself. who gave you appointment to enter my office?

Peace: Ah! Ah! Alhaji. Since when do I need appointment to see you?

Kola: So you no know say the flood don dry. Woo...

Peace: Alhaji, I missed you...

Kola: Ehnnnn! Who do you think you can confuse, or convince and even confiscate with your lie-lie love.

Peace: Why are you talking like this Bobby?

Kola: You see your life? You are calling a typical Yeruba man like me Bobby. With my age size and position you think you can Bobby me? Na lie.

Peace: Sorry. The taxi driver wei bring me com, him name na Bobby.

Kola: Iro! You think I do't know that your bobo wei you dey toss like akara is Bobby. You think you can cook my heart like you cooked his own?

Peace: No vex. I have not seen you for some time now, na him I say make I come find out wetin dey happen.

Kola: Wetin dey happen ke? Wisdom they say it is profitable to direct.

Peace: Alhaji, I call to collect the rent you promised me.

Kola: Rent abi? Tell the people wei send you come say the fly wei enter my eye don comot. Oloriburuku! Leave my office.

Peace: I am not going anywhere. What is the matter with you today?

Kola: Carry your lie-lie love go somewhere. I no do again.

Peace: Okay I hear you. Give me the money make I dey go.

Kola: Which money? Run before I call the security for you.

Peace: Call a battalion of army, I am not going.

Kola: Woo! Let me warm you ke (begins to pack his things). Don't let the security meet you here or the newspapers will read: woman robber shot dead by vigilante.

Peace: Please don't do this to me (she went begging on her knees).

Kola: Since you refuse to go, you can stay
                (leaves her in the office).

End of scene.

Act 4 Scene 4

Glover Road, Saturday afternoon. Two months after Bobby has moved from Ojuelegba. in a moderate sitting room.

Queen: (*Setting the table*) Lunch is served.

Bobby: The aroma is already pulling me like a magnet.

Queen: Your nose must have been fitted with sensors to perceive the aroma from such a distance.

Bobby: I have such a gift for good cooking.

Queen: Stop flattering me.

Bobby: If the truth is synonymous with flattery, (*emerging from within*) let flattery be the language I speak.

Queen: You look sweet in your beach wears.

Bobby: Thanks to you. I cannot trust myself to buy these.

Queen: The credit is all yours for picking the right boutique (*she snuggles close to him for a kiss*).

Bobby: Musa will be here any minute now.

Queen: The picnic basket is packed. I will get dressed right away.

Bobby: (*Takes her in his arms*) we have not decided which beach to go to.

Queen: I will prefer Takwa Bay.

Bobby: Takwa Bay it is then.

Queen: Thanks honey. You are a darling.

Bobby: Thanks for bringing the bloom back to my life.

Queen: Aren't you the one who painted me up in the colours of love.

Bobby: I propose a toast to the eternal freshness of our love.

Queen: I will drink to that.

There is a knock on the door.

Bobby: Musa is already here.

Queen: I will let him in. (*Opens the door*) Hello?

Peace: I am looking for Bobby.

Queen: Who may I say you are?

Peace: Don't bother (*she pushes her way through*)

Bobby: (*Surprised*) Peace? How did you get this place?

Peace: Oh! You thought by picking your things and running away from the house, you would have succeeded in hiding from me? I can see you have hired a maid, but I don't approve of her. (*To Queen*) you are fired.

Queen (*To Bobby*) what is the meaning of this?

Bobby: I am sorry Queen. I will…

Peace: He has not told you he is married, has he? I am his wife.

Bobby: Peace if you don't get out of here this very minute I will make a mince meat of you.

Peace: It will be nice to see you get violent for once.

Bobby: (*To Queen*) This is the Peace I told you about.

69

Queen:	I thought it was over between the two of you?
Bobby:	It is. (*To Peace*) How did you get this place?
Peace:	Don't worry about that. I came to tell you that the rent is due. And if in two weeks time you don't pay, take notice that I will pack and move into this place.
Bobby:	You can do no such thing.
Peace:	Says who? Anyway, (*opens her handbag*) here you have both water and light bills outstanding since the day you absconded. My mission today is to locate the house. I will be back for the payments.

End.

ABOUT THE AUTHOR

Abiathar Zadok, a Composer, Poet, Playwright and Short-story writer was born in Numan, Adamawa State of Nigeria on the First of April 1971.

An award-winning writer; his published collections of poems include **Sunrise, Mosoto: The Season of Love and We Shall be There. The Child Must Die;** his latest work is expected to be out soon.

Hell Is A Woman is his first play. **Nzeanzo: The Enigma** and **The Wedding** are at various stages of completion.

Abiathar Zadok lives in Abuja with his wife Victoria and three children; Veno, Sapwasa, and Sapwada.